DECODABLE BOOK 6

W9-DJI-895

Harcourt

Orlando   Boston   Dallas   Chicago   San Diego

Visit *The Learning Site!*

www.harcourtschool.com

ISBN 0-15-326686-4

1 2 3 4 5 6 7 8 9 10   197   10 09 08 07 06 05 04 03 02 01

Ordering Options
ISBN 0-15-323767-8 (Collection)
ISBN 0-15-326720-8 (package of 5)

Contents

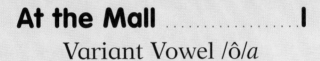

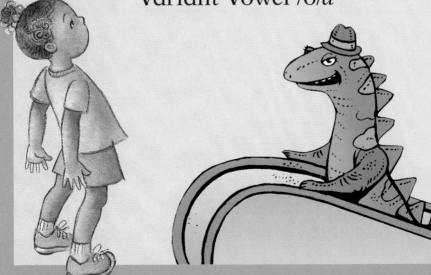

At the Mall

by
Della Rowland

illustrated by
Roger DeMuth

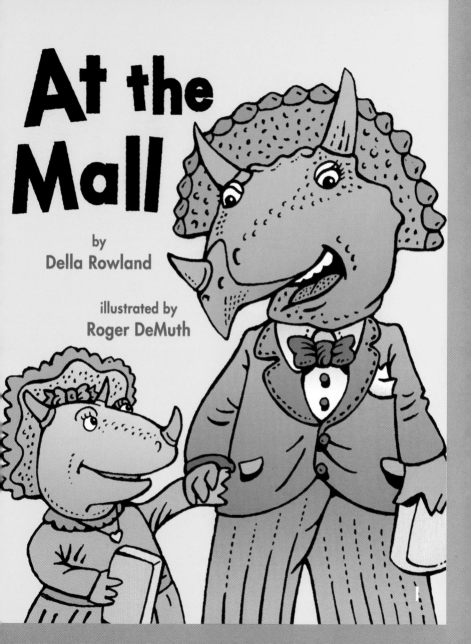

Cass and Dad
are at the mall.

Dad calls to Cass.

Look at all the caps!
Pick, Cass. Pick a cap.

4

Cass is too small.
Cass is sad.

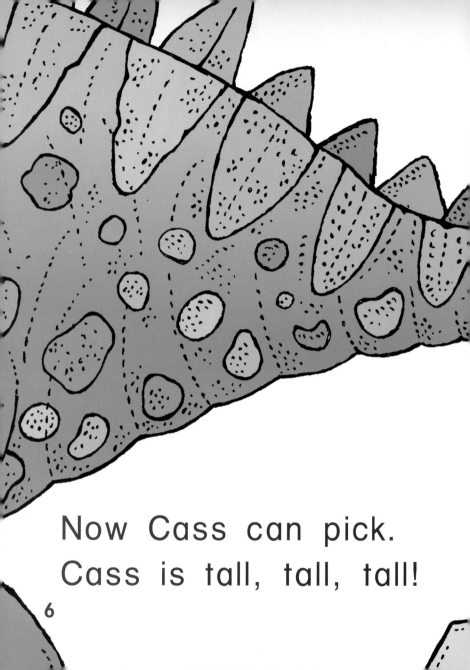

Now Cass can pick.
Cass is tall, tall, tall!

Cass picks a cap.

Cass picked a nap cap!

Tall,
Small,
Tall

by Petra Ortmann

illustrations by
Holly Cooper

Dad is tall.

Kim is not tall at all.
Kim is small.

Dad hops on a wall.
Now Dad is tall,
tall, tall!

Kim is small,
small, small!

Now Kim is on the wall.
Kim will not fall.

Dad helps Kim hop
off the wall.

Now Kim is tall,
tall, tall!

At the Mall

Word Count: 49

High-Frequency Words

are
look
now
the
to
too

Decodable Words*

a	sad
all	**small**
at	**tall**
calls	
can	
cap	
caps	
Cass	
Dad	
is	
mall	
nap	
pick	
picked	
picks	

*Words with /ô/*a* appear in **boldface** type.

Tall, Small, Tall

Word Count: 54

High-Frequency Words

now
the

Decodable Words*

a
all
at
Dad
fall
hop
hops
is
Kim
not
off
on
small
tall
wall
will

*Words with /ô/a appear in **boldface** type.